T0193950

MAMA

Tales of a Middle Aged Martial Artist

NEKO BUDO

BALBOA.
PRESS
A DIVISION OF HAY HOUSE

Balboa Press books may be ordered through booksellers or by contacting:

Balboa Press
A Division of Hay House
1663 Liberty Drive
Bloomington, IN 47403
www.balboapress.com
1 (877) 407-4847

Because of the dynamic nature of the Internet, any web addresses or
links contained in this book may have changed since publication and
may no longer be valid. The views expressed in this work are solely those
of the author and do not necessarily reflect the views of the publisher,
and the publisher hereby disclaims any responsibility for them.

The author of this book does not dispense medical advice or prescribe the use
of any technique as a form of treatment for physical, emotional, or medical
problems without the advice of a physician, either directly or indirectly. The
intent of the author is only to offer information of a general nature to help
you in your quest for emotional and spiritual well-being. In the event you use
any of the information in this book for yourself, which is your constitutional
right, the author and the publisher assume no responsibility for your actions.

Any people depicted in stock imagery provided by Getty Images are
models, and such images are being used for illustrative purposes only.
Certain stock imagery © Getty Images.

Print information available on the last page.

ISBN: 978-1-9822-2901-6 (sc)
ISBN: 978-1-9822-2902-3 (e)

Library of Congress Control Number: 2019906499

Balboa Press rev. date: 06/11/2019

CONTENTS

ACKNOWLEDGEMENTS

I first of all want to thank Sensei Joseph Williams[1] who inspired me to finally write this book, and Sensei Benson who helped me with some spelling questions. I would also like to thank all the senseis who have taught me over the years, both those mentioned in this book, and those whose names I did not mention. Thanks are due to Hanshi Bob Hudson and Hanshi Tom Roberts for helping everyone in Shorei Goju Ryu through a difficult transition. I want to thank my children for allowing me to write about them. And of course, I want to thank Hanshi Frank Blair, who started me on the Path of Shorei Goju Ryu. We miss you, Hanshi.

---

[1] All names and locations have been changed to protect the innocent.

INTRODUCTION

Many books have been written about the martial arts, and many people have written about their experiences in the martial arts. Most of those people are much higher ranking than I am, most are much more experienced, and most of them started at a much younger age than I did. Many of those authors are also men. I decided to write this book to document my experiences, so far, as someone who started her martial arts journey when she was forty years old, and a mother to a small child. I wanted to offer my views from this somewhat unusual (for the martial arts) perspective. I hope that other women, and men, who are over forty can read it and be encouraged to learn and grow in the martial arts community. I also wanted to document my experiences as a student of Hanshi Frank Blair, who we tragically lost on November 20, 2015. Those of us lucky enough to train under Hanshi will never forget him. Thank you, Hanshi.

CHAPTER 1

IN THE BEGINNING

Once upon a time and a very good time it was[2] there was a girl who had just started fifth grade at Robert Kennedy Junior High School in Dix Hills, New York. Every day on the way home from school she walked by a karate dojo and wished she could join and learn karate. It would not happen, at least not now. Her life was controlled by her mother and the refrain of "no money." Besides, her mother also felt "that's not for girls" and even worse "that's not for people like us."

Time passed, as it tends to do. The girl was in high school now. She had a friend whose father owned a dojo (not the one she passed on her way home, but still close). Again she asked. Now the answer was "well you can use your COLLEGE MONEY if you want." Now she was too scared because she had discovered that her mother had saved a ridiculously small amount of money for her college education. She knew that her life was going to be very

---

[2] James Joyce, Portrait of the Artist as a Young Man, pg.1 BW Huebsch, Inc. 1922

difficult and she was afraid to spend that money. So, once again, karate would have to wait.

Years passed. She criss-crossed the eastern half of the country. Her heart was badly broken several times. She worked hard. Finally she ended up in Illinois against her will. She was married and had a 1 1/2 year old daughter. One day, in the mail, she received a newsletter from a local hospital advertising a women's self defense seminar. She convinced her (extremely cheap) husband to let her sign up for her fortieth birthday present. She didn't know it yet, but that day would change her life.

So, obviously the girl was me. I could write a whole different book about how I ended up in Illinois. The short version is that I'm a DO. A doctor of osteopathic medicine. New York was, at least in the 80's, still a small DO state. Not too many of us. So, when I ended up doing a rotation in Missouri, it was like Osteopathic Nirvana! No explaining myself at every turn, no crazy hospitals refusing to let us touch patients. We had our OWN hospitals, thank you very much! Even though I tried to go back to the east coast, mostly to try and please other people, after that 6 week rotation it was hard to again tolerate the overt discrimination DOs faced there. Eventually I did get married, in Missouri, and after my first child was born three years later I was dragged against my will to Illinois for a job opportunity for my husband. About 6 months after that I went to the self defense seminar given at Frank Blair's Karate and I met Hanshi Frank Blair.

It was a four hour seminar, and after the first two hours I KNEW I wanted to sign up for regular classes. There was no way I would be able to retain all the information I was getting without regular practice and instruction so I could get everything right. And I wanted to learn MORE! I love to learn new things, and especially things I'm interested in. So I really set out to convince my husband that I wanted to do this. Unbelievably, he agreed. Honestly, the cost of signing up for regular lessons was not inconsequential. And I heard a bajillion times from him over the following years about how it shouldn't cost MONEY to learn and the Master should teach in return for cleaning the dojo, etc. Well, that's the way it is now. The rent and taxes need to be paid at the dojo besides electricity and other utilities. Luckily, he is somewhat interested in martial arts; he did some Kung Fu growing up. And I think he secretly believed I would give up and it would be something else he could harass me about. So, after YEARS of haranguing me about not having any physical activity (besides chasing around a toddler, which didn't count to him) he acquiesced.

They say that "when the student is ready, the master appears" and that is pretty much how it happened for me. I was working part time reading sleep studies because I wanted to be with my daughter. For physicians, "full time" means ALL the time and we both couldn't do that unless we had some sort of 24 hour daycare available. So, I FINALLY had some time for karate after literally decades of working around the clock and being on call. Of course it wasn't totally easy either. My husband was on call intermittently, and let's just say that he didn't LOVE taking care of a small child. I had no family or friends in the area. I was pretty isolated. But it was something I had wanted to do for a very long time. Obviously, going through about 15 years of medical training, I was also used to "delayed gratification." So I kept at it and slowly I progressed. After my daughter started preschool two half days a week it got a little easier as there were morning classes at the dojo as well as evenings.

CHAPTER 2

SEE WITHOUT LOOKING, HEAR WITHOUT LISTENING

In any case, I went that day. It was in February 2001, and I remember the weather wasn't the greatest. I didn't know EXACTLY where it was and in those days before GPS and Google maps, I got lost. Thankfully I DID have a cell phone and I remember calling the dojo and being guided in by Sensei West. There were about five women in total, including myself. I remember Hanshi giving us a brief lecture about personal safety and being aware. That's the first time I heard him say the phrase "See without looking, hear without listening." I think this is now my personal motto and I tell my two daughters this all the time. I think they're sick of hearing it but it really is an important concept. It basically just means to be alert. And no headphones when you're outside walking or running! In fact, when I dropped off Natalie (my older daughter) for her freshman year at college, the last thing I said to her (or rather shouted to her) as she walked away was "SEE WITHOUT LOOKING, HEAR WITHOUT LISTENING!"

After the lecture came the physical part of the seminar. At first it was just basic punching and kicking but then we got into wrist locks, arm bars, chokes, leg locks, and what Hanshi called "floor strategies." I can't remember if we did any throws or immobilizations. "Floor strategies," it turned out, was a euphemism for rape prevention. At first I was a bit shocked and I was thinking "Argh! I didn't know I'd have strangers sitting on me!" So, it was shocking, but then I realized, "Hey, this is what I came for." So I just put the shock aside and tried to concentrate on learning the escapes. And somewhere during all this is when I realized I NEEDED to sign up for regular lessons if I was going to remember anything.

I was allowed to try out the regular lessons for a few weeks before I officially signed up. I have to say, out of the five women who came for the seminar, I was the only one who signed up for regular lessons. That makes me either really smart, or really crazy. I think I'm more a combination of those two things. At that time, I was only able to come once a week because of where we were living and my husband's call schedule. I was told years later that everyone thought that I would quit after a few months because of my weekly attendance, and also because during one of my first lessons I got punched full in the face. But it really wasn't lack of interest that kept me from coming more often, just circumstances.

When I finally DID officially sign up I was given my first gi and I was SO HAPPY. Of course, I'm undertall and have short stubby arms and legs so I had to hem everything.

But I was still really happy. I spent several hours in front of the bathroom mirror in our rented townhome practicing tying my belt correctly while my daughter watched me. I didn't want to come to class with it tied WRONG! I was so happy and proud when I had it figured out!

Another big moment was when I finally memorized the roundhouse block. That took me a couple of weeks also. Slowly I was progressing and I finally made it from white belt to gold belt. It was somewhere during that time that a devastating event occurred. I suffered my first, and most difficult, miscarriage.

I had gone to my new OB/GYN in Chicago, since we had moved less than a year prior from Missouri. Just for a routine first check up and ultrasound. And my happiness turned to anguish when I learned there was no heartbeat. The fetus was dead. After that horrible day there were a series of more horrible days. I had to have a D&C to remove the dead fetus. It was terrible. A few days later it was Saturday. Should I go to karate? I was trying to decide. Finally, I said to my husband, "I'm going." So, still bleeding, I went to try to take my mind off everything. It was to set a pattern that I continue to the present day. Karate as therapy.

After that I continued to make very slow progress. We had been house hunting before the miscarriage and I had found a neighborhood I liked. And what a coincidence, it was pretty close to the dojo! I wanted to drop the whole idea after the miscarriage; I just didn't feel like it anymore. But my husband wanted to continue and we ended up buying a house. After we moved in, going to karate got easier. Then when my daughter started in preschool two half days a week, I began to progress much more rapidly. I did have another miscarriage but this time I didn't need the D&C. Still devastating though. Again used karate as therapy. Then finally in late 2002 I became pregnant again and this time everything was going OK even though I felt like I was going to be holding my breath for the whole nine months. I knew I had to tell Hanshi because at some point it would be obvious and now that I was a brown belt there were certain things that really weren't a good idea to be doing while pregnant.

CHAPTER 3

OBSTETRICS AND PEDIATRICS

So I did tell Hanshi. I remember his shocked expression when I told him I had suffered not one but TWO miscarriages. I hastily added that neither one had ANYTHING to do with karate (because they didn't). I BEGGED him not to make me quit. That would have made me crazy. I needed something else to think about. So, we agreed I would do kata (forms) and limited self defense. Sparring was out, but that was fine with me because I have never been a big fan of sport sparring. It went surprisingly well, and all the instructors and my fellow students seemed to be OK with it. I don't think anyone before me had continued throughout their pregnancy at Hanshi's dojos. In fact, I think it helped during labor and delivery. I remember it didn't take very long. Also, I think my mental health was helped quite a bit by continuing. Karate is a community, and a dojo is like a family. I had the community's support during a stressful time. After Sara was born, I remember her first outing when she was a few days old was to see her older sister, Natalie, graduate in her Little Dragons class.

I should probably explain the concept of Little Dragons. When children reach the age of three years old, they are allowed to start karate in the Little Dragons. This is a special class for the ages of three to five years old. Natalie had started about a year before Sara was born, and I always helped out with that class. Honestly, it was a little like herding cats. If you could get them to all stand still on the class formation line for thirty seconds, you were doing really well. But at that age, they LOVE being with Mama, and Natalie really loved doing the class because I was with her. Not like now, when I think she would rather eat lint than do anything with me. But usually I can convince her to come with me for a class or two when she's home on break from college. I think one of our more memorable events at the dojo was when we did the "Karate Car Wash" to try and recruit some new students. It was in the parking lot of the dojo and I remember Natalie in her Little Dragons uniform handing out brochures from the dojo. She was super cute and people were happy to talk to her and ask her if she liked karate. Fortunately she still LOVED it and was super enthusiastic in her responses. It's still a very happy memory for me.

I had graduated to "apprentice" Shodan, or first degree black belt before Sara was born. Every December we have the Extravaganza, during which you lose the "apprentice" designation and assume your full rank. Luckily, I had about five months in between Sara's birth and the Extravaganza.

I usually describe the Extravaganza as a family reunion but with stress and sweating. Basically you have to perform all your material for your new black belt rank, in front of a "Board" consisting of the Masters (including Hanshi, who is the Grand Master) and other black belts who are not graduating that year. A second degree (Nidan) requires one year in grade after Shodan. A third degree (Sandan) requires two years, a fourth degree (Yondan) three years, a fifth degree (Godan) four years, a sixth degree (Rokudan) five years, and so on up to tenth degree. All the schools in our style (Shorei Goju Ryu) attend with their graduating black belts, and you get to see all the people that maybe you haven't seen for the entire year. It is a lot of fun in some ways, but stressful if you are graduating.

Natalie eventually "aged out" of little dragons, and she was able to go to Junior Shodan when she was 6 years old. We used to designate the under 16 year old students as "Junior." In any case, I think I enjoyed it more than she did, but at that age they are super adorable when they go through their kata and other material. She was so PROUD, and so was I. I remember that I bought her a special black belt and we had her name and the style name embroidered on it. She was so HAPPY when she saw that belt. Sensei West had to help me out to get it. He took it down to the mysterious "Ben Enterprises" to have it embroidered. I was still getting lost around the area on a regular basis so I didn't trust myself to get it done. I'm still so grateful he did it for me. When people tried to tell me where it was, it sounded like, "over the river, through the woods, left at the cow, right at the barn."

My younger child, Sara, had been watching her sister and I do karate since she was born so when she started Little Dragons she was READY. She was actually about two years and ten months old when she started and she was so excited. I always said, "Sara has been doing karate since she was a FETUS," and I had actually signed her up for lessons when she was about six months old. Sensei West was having a "bad" month regarding signing up new students. I just remember I offered to sign Sara up immediately IF I could get a "deal." I can't remember now exactly what the "deal" was, but Sara ended up being the youngest student ever signed up for lessons at Frank Blair's Karate! Of course, she could not actually start classes yet. Since she could crawl she wanted to be on that mat, and I think she could hardly believe it when she was finally allowed to be in a class! And of course Natalie and I helped out with her classes too so that made it even better. I encourage all families to learn karate together because it is so enjoyable. Especially when the children are younger because that is the time when they LOVE to do things with their parents. Once they get older, the magic is gone and they don't like being together as much. I really miss those years now when we were together at the dojo so much. Especially now, that Natalie is at college and Sara seems to be having a "crisis of faith" as we used to call it when I was growing up. At least, that's what we called it as Catholics. She doesn't want anything to do with karate currently. I've been told that many people come back to it later in life, and I've met a few who did, so hopefully Sara will too.

We often talk about the "what if" questions people ask in class. As in "what if an attacker does this or that?" Obviously instructors try to answer these questions. I remember learning club self defense. We are taught that once you disarm an attacker with a club (a stick of any kind, like a golf club, etc.) you cannot turn around and use the club on your attacker because then if someone saw it they might think YOU were the aggressor (and I SUPPOSE it's morally and ethically wrong). Of course, I had Natalie and Sara was in a baby carrier. So I would ask, "what if I am with my two children? I can't run fast. What then? I need to make sure the attacker can't follow me." After a few times asking, Sensei West said "I think if someone saw a mom with two kids, one in a baby carrier, that person would not assume that you would pick a fight with anyone." Other senseis have agreed. Women have a little more latitude in these matters, especially when they have children.

CHAPTER 4

ORTHOPEDICS

My karate life has not been totally smooth. I should state first of all, that when the OB/GYN tells you to take off 6-8 weeks before resuming karate? LISTEN TO THEM. Even if you feel ok. Your ligaments will be all stretched out and you will be prone to injury. After Sara was born I was itching to get back to karate. It was my second time (giving birth, I mean), and it wasn't nearly as bad as the first time. After two weeks or so I said "I feel FINE. I'm going to class!" Everything was going great until we started to drill jump spinning back kicks. I remember jumping and spinning while thinking "This is going great!" Then I landed. Later, people told me they heard the CRACK noise across the dojo. I crumpled to the floor, and I watched in pain and horror as my right ankle started to swell immediately. I tried to get up and couldn't. Someone helped me to the chairs lined up at the edge of the mat that were there for parents and other spectators. I put my foot up and my ankle was starting to look really bad as we put ice packs on it.

After the class finished, I had to be half carried out to my car. Driving home was HILARIOUS with my ankle killing me. I was really happy that we got the house near the dojo, that's for sure! It was so bad I was using my bo (six foot long staff) to hobble around and I couldn't climb the stairs. Being physicians, we would both rather DIE than go to the ER but by the next day we had no choice. We had two small children and my husband had to go to work. So we went and luckily it wasn't broken but I had apparently ripped out most of the ligaments. They wrapped it up and back home we went. I slowly improved and I went for a follow up with the orthopedic surgeon. Now I'm sure that there are some good orthopedic people who aren't like the one I met and I knew some good people in Missouri. But I was in Illinois. I was told to "find another sport." Sometimes, if you are older and overweight, orthopedic people don't take your problems that seriously. Especially if there is no surgery to be done. So I remember I told him that it took me FORTY YEARS to find a "sport" that I enjoyed, and I did NOT want to give it up. And secondly, karate is not a "sport." Our style, Shorei Goju Ryu is often translated as "Graceful Beautiful Hard Soft Way." It's the WAY, a way of life, a philosophy, NOT a "sport." Finally, he gave up and I ended up with a lace up ankle brace. The ankle brace was for AFTER I spent (I believe) six weeks wearing the cursed "boot." I hated the boot. In case you have never experienced it, it is a big metal and Velcro contraption that goes up to just below your knee. It's heavy and annoying. Especially when you have to carry a baby in a car seat. Ugh. I think that now there are some made of plastic which I am sure is lighter.

Anyway, after I went back (with the lace up ankle brace) everything was OK for a while. Of course, I was back to my very limited attendance since now I had Sara and I couldn't go back to the morning classes yet. I was trying to learn my material to go to second degree, or Nidan, and it was taking me way longer than the minimum of one year. A few months after I started back at the dojo, I was in a big hurry at home and I was trying to find a sled in the garage (it was winter) and I fell down the stairs and CRACK, I turned the LEFT ankle over and it started swelling immediately. I was more angry at myself than anything else.

After my husband got home it was back to the ER, more X-Rays and thankfully again nothing was broken but the ligaments again were torn. Again the dang boot. This time though, I couldn't stand the no karate thing and I went back with the boot. I talked about it with Sensei West and Hanshi and my feeling was "If I can walk, I can do kata" and luckily they agreed with me. I did as much as I could, and people began to say the boot was my "secret weapon" after I accidentally whacked them with it.

After the six weeks in the boot I got another lace up ankle brace for the left ankle. I've been using them ever since. But that wasn't the end of my orthopedic issues. At some point I injured one knee doing a side kick, and the other at home kneeling on a bed. With my history of unpleasant encounters with orthopedic surgeons I took matters into my own hands. I knew that once they start doing arthroscopies on your knees to remove bits of ripped cartilage, you are starting down the slippery slope to knee replacement. Sometimes, also, it's bad when you know all the possible things that can go wrong during and after surgery. I bought two big knee braces with metal strips on the sides to prevent any lateral movement. So basically now when I go to karate I'm kind of encased in armor over my knees and ankles. However, it works for me and I've been able to progress in my knowledge.

I've also at various times injured myself outside of karate. I hurt my right elbow yanking a trash can that was frozen into the ground. Smart. And in 2015 I injured the left ankle AGAIN falling down the stairs in our house. Ugh. I tried to get away with not wearing the boot and I ended up seeing a podiatrist (I'm pretty much DONE with orthopedic surgeons) after it wasn't getting better. Again, ligaments ripped out. I should have known what was coming when he asked "What's your favorite color?" "Blue!" I replied happily. Then out came the casting materials. I remember saying "Oh no! Not the CAST!" But he was adamant since I wasn't cooperating with the BOOT I was getting the CAST to immobilize the ankle. Double UGH. That was not fun, especially trying to take a shower. That was in 2015 and thankfully I haven't had any major orthopedic issues since. But when you have an injury you have to just do what you can. Luckily I've been at dojos with senseis who understand that it's better to do SOME karate and work around your injuries than to give up altogether. Also, being a middle aged martial artist you have to accept that you can't do the same things as a 20 year old. But as my current sensei (Sensei Williams) says, "Youth and speed must be replaced by age and TREACHERY." I love that saying and it pretty much says it all.

CHAPTER 5

ONCOLOGY

So my two children and I were progressing in our respective ranks. Sensei West left to start his own dojo. We kind of went through an instructor go round for a while. Then Hanshi decided to close our dojo due to rent/taxes being really high where we were and we transferred to his other dojo about five miles away. (He initially had three when we started, now he was down to two.)

I had been having what my husband calls "womanly problems" since shortly after I had Sara at the age of 42. Believe me when I tell you, having a baby after 42 is not for wimps but I really wanted her and adore her. Anyway, I was having a lot of what is called "abnormal uterine bleeding." Now, Natalie calls anything in the pre-internet era "the dark times" and I can tell you truthfully that in the dark times I would have had a hysterectomy and moved on with my life. But by 2009 the insurance companies were starting to run the show thanks to obamacare and it wasn't so simple anymore.

I'd been to the OB/GYN of course, and had numerous painful and unpleasant "diagnostic procedures." I was told I wasn't anemic "enough" to qualify for a hysterectomy. I was pretty miserable. Finally, in early 2009, I had an episode where I was bleeding for over six weeks. Not heavily, but annoying. I had MORE labs drawn, hormone levels, and an EXTREMELY painful uterine biopsy. Again the talk about "you're experiencing perimenopause, just get used to it." THANKS. And the phone call from some assistant, "Your labs are FINE, you don't have cancer." In the exasperated, sarcastic tone. Then the biopsy results came back. Endometrial cancer.

My world came crashing down. I had surgery soon after. Everything out. Then another bomb: One lymph node had a microscopic metastasis. I remember running upstairs and throwing up because I knew all the horrible things that were in my immediate future. I was just recovering from the surgery and now I had to start chemotherapy. Three rounds, once a month. Then daily radiation for about eight weeks, then three more rounds of chemotherapy. With two children ages six and ten. Away from family. I was just starting back at the dojo when I got the news that I needed the chemo and radiation. I remember someone asking me how I was and just bursting into tears at the front desk. But it had to be done. I remember the first chemo session (each one was all day long) and thinking "goodbye hair!" A few weeks later I got the intense itchy/sore feeling all over my scalp while I was at the grocery store. I had been warned that this meant it would start falling out soon.

I had prepared myself. I had a wig, and a bunch of scarves. I just remember one day after a morning karate class coming home and taking off my ponytail elastic and thinking, "why does it look like my hair GREW?" Then I realized that obviously it hadn't grown. The tension of the ponytail had dislodged a big wad of hair. Sure enough I pulled gently and a massive chunk of hair came off into my hand. Horror. I pulled off as much as I could before I took a shower. By the weekend, my husband just shaved off what was left. I found out that the wigs were HOT and ITCHY. Karate posed a problem at first. The scarves weren't that secure and the wig was out of the question. I finally found something that had some elastic in the back and it was a little better. I had a black one and a white one with Chinese characters on it for graduations (when we had to wear the white gi).

It was a struggle, that's for sure. And I found out that restless legs syndrome was nothing to laugh about. I was, as I said before, reading sleep studies part time. I was board certified in Internal Medicine, Pulmonary, and Sleep Disorders. We always thought "restless legs, how bad can it be?" Well, restless legs was a side effect of the chemotherapy and it was bad. I ended up on medication just to get it to ease up enough to sleep a little. Plus, as usual, I was hauling the two children to school and back. Speaking of sleep disorders, it was about the time I had surgery that the sleep lab I was reading for closed due to obamacare. Everyone lost their jobs. I decided not to worry about it then and just concentrate on surviving the cancer. Because having metastatic cancer is nothing to take lightly, even if it's just microscopic mets. I thought I might die. Especially after one visit to the oncologist when he announced "You are such a GREAT CASE that we had a Grand Rounds about you!"

Now, anyone in the medical field knows that you don't want to be a "great case" and certainly you don't want to be the subject of a Grand Rounds! Both of these things usually mean you are doomed. I remember I gasped and then burst into tears. He apologized immediately and he told me "I forgot that you know what that means!" I know he meant well, and that "normal" people probably are very happy to hear they were the subject of a Grand Rounds, but for me it was obviously horrifying. I figured I would be dead in a year.

After the first three rounds of chemo I had a "break" before the radiation and it happened to be the beginning of the summer break at school. The radiation techs told me, "If you want to go somewhere, do it now" so we took off for Montreal so my kids could bother people in French. They were both attending an international school and were in a French immersion program. It was pretty horrible travelling with the wig and the scarves. I wasn't feeling that great either. Somehow I dragged myself through Montreal and we drove back. Then the radiation started.

Everyone has heard the phrase, "praying for death." Well, during those eight weeks I learned what that meant. And afterwards, the radiology techs told me that many other people also told them that. However, they try not to mention it to patients before they start their radiation "journey." At first it's not too bad but then the pain and the diarrhea start. And then you're vomiting blood, having bloody diarrhea, and you are in constant pain. I remember one morning drinking orange juice, feeling it hit my stomach, and vomiting it back out into the kitchen sink. That was one of the few days I could not physically make it to karate. But usually I would try my best to get there. That was the time period when I used to have fantasies about one of my fellow Middle Aged Martial Artists beheading me with a samurai sword. I knew he had one and I kept thinking, would he get in trouble legally if I left a letter stating that I had asked him to behead me? I felt like I was ready to go. If I didn't have two little children to take care of, I probably would have found a way to make it happen.

It was during the summer and I remember on Tuesday and Thursday there were morning classes at the dojo. I would pack up the kids in their karate gis, and drive to the radiation center. My husband would meet me there and watch them for the time I was getting irradiated. After I was done, I took them and drove to the dojo. We would be late but we would be able to have about an hour or so of lessons. I had approved it before hand with the senseis and Hanshi, of course. Sometimes it was pretty brutal on me. The other days of the week I had them in morning day care so I would just drop them off, go get irradiated, come back and pick them up. This also took some arranging but I had been using this particular daycare for years. And luckily in the summers they had a "camp" program so even though my older daughter was 10 years old she could stay for the camp as kind of a "helper" with the littler kids. I was so grateful to the director.

I remember for the last week or so of the radiation I couldn't take it anymore and I just stopped eating so I could avoid some of the bloody diarrhea and vomiting. I was really wishing for death during that time. And honestly, I thought that I WAS going to die. I remember that at that time you could hold birthday parties at the dojo for a fee. The senseis helped get pizza and they did a mini lesson for the birthday child and their friends. Since both of my children were born in July, I always held conjoint parties for them. It was just so much easier and I really did feel like I was going to die so I had their party that year at the dojo. They had a good time and so did their friends. At least I think so.

I have mentioned previously how my husband is less than supportive. I remember when I went to find out when my radiation appointments were being scheduled (THEY tell YOU when you're coming, not vice versa) he went on about "You tell them you're coming in the morning!" Because that's when the camp was, and it would be easier for HIM. So obviously, they had me scheduled in the afternoons. I remember bursting into tears and begging them for a morning appointment. The appointments were every weekday, five days a week. So it wasn't that easy. They had to call and move some people around and I'm eternally grateful to whoever those people were. I'm not sure I could have done it otherwise.

After that hell on earth, there were three more cycles of the chemotherapy and then finally I was done around Halloween. It took me a few months to recover. I remember going to the Extravaganza that year still with my headscarf on. Either at one of our dojo graduations or the Extravaganza (I can't remember now) Hanshi recognized me for continuing to go to class through the whole ordeal. The thing is, I am not sure I would have made it through without going to karate. I needed something else to think about, just as I did during my second pregnancy after the miscarriages.

CHAPTER 6

NEPHROLOGY AND THE "NUT"

After the Year of Cancer was over, I tried to find another job in Sleep Disorders. Thanks at least in part to obamacare, that didn't work out. The number of positions plummeted as the insurance industry started the drive to eliminate most in-lab studies and the resulting rise of patients having to do sleep studies in their home, unmonitored. These, of course, were not nearly as accurate since you can't monitor as many things and when leads fall off, well that's too bad because the patient is ALONE. So, I started to look for part time work in urgent care centers. I had run an ER at night for a year and a half. Near Detroit. But by that time they only wanted NPs and PAs. Even when I volunteered to work for the salary of an NP it didn't matter. You see, physicians are trained for maybe 12 years or more, and part of it is training to think for ourselves and to do what is RIGHT, not what is cheaper for the insurance company or the hospital. We are not there to make money for the CEO. So, we are not obedient and therefore not wanted. I didn't want to go back to full time pulmonology because of the two kids and full time basically means ALL THE TIME with people calling you and paging you at all hours. And frankly, I wasn't sure I could do it any more. So, after a while, and Mr. Supportive telling me repeatedly that "No one wants YOU anymore!" I thought, well, I'll throw myself into karate then.

I went to the dojo as often as I could and I started graduating on time. Of course it wasn't easy but one of my best qualities is persistence. I may not be strong or flexible anymore, but by sheer persistence I learned and progressed.

During this same time, we had been monitoring my husband's renal function. When our first child was born, we thought "Hey, better get some life insurance!" because I only had a small policy which my mother made me take out when I first moved to Missouri. This was, in her words, "In case you die I'll have to ship your body home." Thanks MA. Anyway, when we were trying to get life insurance, we had to have labs drawn. Mine were fine, but his showed some elevation of his renal function studies. As to why, all he could remember is when he was a young teenager he had maybe a strep infection and started having hematuria. It resolved, but perhaps some damage was done at that time. We may never know for sure. In any case, we started monitoring it and his renal function slowly worsened. By 2010 he had to have a shunt inserted for possible dialysis in the future. I remember I was still wearing the headscarf when that happened as my hair hadn't grown in enough to go without it. We kept hoping his renal status would stabilize but it, along with his mood, progressively worsened.

By then we had all been victims of his intermittent "harangues" which lasted about 45 minutes once he got started. I remember Sara timed him and that's how we got the 45 minute figure. He had always had sort of a Jekyll and Hyde personality. I married Dr. Jekyll and Dr. Jekyll was always out at work, but I met Mr. Hyde just before my older daughter was born. It was quite shocking and I hoped it was a one-time event. It was not. The harangues increased in frequency. Everything I did or thought was WRONG. My (Italian) cooking was "killing" the children. So I stopped cooking. They lived on chicken nuggets and mac and cheese. Anything I could make and clean up quickly before he got home. I used to crochet. I was wasting money on yarn. I had to quit that too. There were a lot of things, but the one thing I wouldn't quit was karate. So, that became a focus of the harangues.

I should mention that many people with chronic diseases like renal failure develop very … difficult personalities. In fact, during my medical training renal failure patients (along with a few other diseases that I won't mention) were notorious for being difficult. Now I have met some very nice and kind people with chronic diseases but unfortunately my husband was living up to the stereotype of renal failure patients. A disease which involves painful procedures, frequent lengthy treatments, and the only hope is a transplant. He went on the transplant list around the beginning of 2011. His labs continued to worsen and eventually we had to start dialysis. At home. Thanks to obamacare (again), unless you are very elderly or sick, you have to do this at home now. They bring in all the equipment, hook it up to a bathroom sink, and provide you with a big binder of instructions. Thank God, a nurse comes in to help you the first few times. After that, you are left on your own. Four afternoons a week I had to pick up the kids from school, race home, and help him get hooked up. He did most of the set up before I got there. It was about four hours each session, I think. Surprisingly, he left Wednesdays open so we (the kids and I) could go to black belt class. It was a difficult time, but at least while he was getting the dialysis treatment he was unable to follow me around haranguing me. And when we were done and I had disconnected him and cleaned up he was usually too tired to start in on me and he went to bed. The bad part was if the alarms started ringing on the machine he would get hysterical screaming until the problem was fixed. Sometimes I had to call the nurses to get it sorted and he was freaking out the whole time, which did not help. It was during that time that he began referring to me as "stupid" and "useless." And of course his favorite, "idiot." Frequently. The harangues have been described by the children as "verbal whippings" or "verbal beatings" and I think that's accurate. So, obviously karate was a real escape for us. The most difficult part of all was being tied to the house for someone who was so hateful and mean. We couldn't be away for more than a couple of days because we had to do the dialysis. I remember I had to miss my father's funeral in New York because of Mr. Hyde.

Occasionally, the kids had friends over and I was always on edge about that. He preferred to stay up in his "lair" on the second floor in what we called the TV room where he had his big TV. Incidentally, that's also where all the dialysis equipment was set up.

So, one day, Sara's best friend from karate came over with his mom and dad. The kids were all playing together and the parents were sitting at the kitchen table. We were chatting about different things, and as the mom does karate too, the talk drifted toward the dojo. Off goes my husband on one of his anti-karate harangues. I tried to stop him but he paid no attention to me, of course. "Hanshi doesn't know anything. He's not teaching you guys 'real karate.'" And on and on he went for the usual 45 minutes or so. Now, the mom in question had been a student of Hanshi's for much longer than me, maybe 25 to 30 years. I saw her mouth drop open in disbelief at what she was hearing. And I knew that now everyone would know what I was living with.

Sure enough, the next time we go in, someone wheels around and says "Hey, I hear you're married to a total NUT!" I cringed a little, then I went to apologize to Hanshi because he knew too now. I told him that was NOT how we felt about him, and obviously I did NOT share my husband's views. Thankfully he was very understanding and he said he knew we (Natalie, Sara, and myself) did not think like that. But from then on, everyone in Shorei Goju Ryu world knew about my husband "the nut." Once, someone even told me I was a "hero" because often people would quit because their spouse was unsupportive, and I was living with "outright HOSTILITY!" But I didn't think I was a hero, I just was very persistent. But at least now no one has asked me about "the NUT" lately, although I have had people ask me if I'm still married to "that GUY."

Finally, around Memorial Day of 2014, we got the call that a kidney was available. It was about 8:00 pm. We rushed into the hospital, got him checked in, then I took the kids home. The next day I went and checked on him, but he was still asleep from the anesthesia and he didn't know I was there. The next few days were just getting the kids to school, checking on him, picking them up and going home. Ironically, one of my best karate friends, Sensei Baylor, was a pharmacist at the same hospital. She said she was going to check in on him and I warned her about his "anti-karate" tirades. I didn't want to lose another friend. Fortunately, she is a very tough, high-ranking instructor and she told me if he started in on her she was going to cut off his pain meds! Luckily, I think he was really scared of her and he never uttered one peep out of line.

After he was discharged (really soon, in my opinion), he mostly stayed in bed or his lair and didn't bother us too much. However, he did have to go back to the hospital a couple of times for infections. He is fairly stable now, and it's been about five years since the transplant with no rejection, although of course he has to remain on anti-rejection medications for life.

CHAPTER 7

GASTROENTEROLOGY

Unfortunately, I had started to develop side effects from my cancer treatment a few years before the transplant occurred. It started with falafels. If I ate one I had progressive pain and stomach cramping and it didn't end until I vomited it out, usually the next day after a night of hell. Then bread was an issue, then pasta (that was a severe blow, believe me). It got worse and worse over time. At the worst, I could only eat puddings, soup with no solids in it, and other liquids. At the same time, my mild lactose intolerance became extreme, and remains so to this day. I lost about 50 pounds (not that I didn't need to lose the weight!) In the winter, every time I pulled off my gloves, my wedding ring fell off. The staff at the local grocery store asked me to please get a smaller size since I had to ask someone to fetch it from under a display or shelf several times! Of course, I got no sympathy at home. He told me all the GI specialists in Chicago were idiots and if I wanted to get my bowel perforated, then go ahead! I got more sympathy at the grocery store (it's a smallish one in a large chain) and they frequently voiced their concern. And of course, at karate, where many people noticed my weight loss. And I was absent intermittently because each "episode" could be over 24 hours long, and I would be exhausted afterwards. There would also continue to be minor stomach cramps for several days after. The longest episode was 30 hours before I finally vomited up the offending food. I was miserable and in a lot of pain physically and mentally because I felt that I was married to someone who wished that I would die (but not until he got a transplant and didn't need me anymore, of course!)

Anyway, things came to a head about a month after the transplant. I had been seeing a new internist who thought maybe I had gluten sensitivity. So while she ran some tests, I thought I would try some baby carrots. I started to feel the pain a couple of hours later. Overnight, it kept getting worse. It was a continually escalating, midabdominal cramping pain. For those of you with first aid training, it was right where you put your fist to perform the Heimlich maneuver. I remember it was Saturday around 4:00 pm when I ate the carrots, and the pain started a few hours later. It got worse and worse as I lay in bed writhing around. At around 6 or 7 am he told me I had the take him to the hospital because he had a fever. I slowly got up and made my way to the bathroom. Apparently, I wasn't moving fast enough because he called one of his friends from work to take him instead. OK, I went back to bed. The kids were now 15 and 11, so they were old enough to mostly take care of themselves. The pains were getting worse and worse and by evening I was laying on the bathroom floor retching, trying to get the damn carrots back up. Natalie got scared and called the Nut on his cellphone. In between retching I told him to just leave me be but he ended up calling his BOSS to come to the house. That was, honestly, the LAST thing I wanted. While they were on the way over, at around 10:00 pm, I finally brought up the undigested, chewed up carrots. I remember laying on the bathroom floor in relief. But I had to get through the trial of his boss and his wife coming over. Don't get me wrong, they are very nice people, but I was too weak to get dressed and I remember I threw on a bathrobe. I told them I vomited up what was making me sick but as a physician, I think his boss was somewhat concerned. Apparently I was pale and I know I was diaphoretic. They wanted to take me to the ER, but I didn't want to drag the kids out. They needed to go to bed since the next day was a Monday and they had school. I remember they did ask me why I hadn't seen a GI person. I was leaning against the wall at the top of the stairs and I remember blurting out "Because Kumar (we'll call him) says all the gastroenterologists in Chicago are morons and will perforate my bowel! And I can't go back to Missouri!" He and his wife looked at each other in disbelief. But it was the truth. When people are in pain, or exhausted, often they will just tell the truth because it's easier than making up a lie.

Finally, I did accept their offer to take the kids to school in the morning. I still was having residual cramps but the worst of it was over. I got up in the morning when the boss's wife came and picked them up but then I went to lay back down until pick up time. I had been in pain for about 40 hours and I was totally spent. After the Nut came home (and probably got yelled at by his boss) I finally saw at first a surgeon (because we thought I had a bowel obstruction from the cancer treatment) and then a gastroenterologist.

No obstruction was seen on the CT scan and I was scoped eventually, but nothing was seen. I had gastric emptying studies done, nothing. I can't even remember all the tests I had done. And then the gastroenterologist tried many different medications but nothing was working. Meanwhile I was losing more weight and missing more karate, though I did my best to make sure the kids got to their classes.

Finally the gastroenterologist suggested yet another medication which I was SURE was not going to work but he said "just give it a shot, we don't know why but sometimes it works." So I tried. The problem is that if something doesn't work I pay a heavy price if I eat the "wrong" food. After a couple of weeks on the medication I cautiously began to very slowly expand the diet. Much to my shock, it was working! I've been on it now for a few years and while it's not perfect, things are much better than before. I can't eat everything (bread, regular pasta, and raw vegetables are still off limits for me), but overall things are better. I can eat gluten free pasta, so I'm pretty happy.

CHAPTER 8

AS THE DOJO TURNS...

Sometime around when Sara graduated to black belt in Little Dragons, Hanshi had to close our dojo due to financial reasons (as I mentioned earlier) and we all transferred to his location a few miles further from our house. Of course, no one is happy when they have to move, and neither were we. Now we had more people squished into a narrower space. Since Sensei West left to start his own dojo a few years prior, we had kind of been on a instructor- go-round, and it continued at our new location. It was hardest on the kids because they get attached to an instructor, then a year or so later they would be gone, replaced by yet another person.

I have mentioned Sensei Baylor previously, my karate friend, bunkai partner, and pharmacist. Sometime before 2011, we became saddled with a chief instructor that I could tolerate, but she absolutely hated. Actually "hated" is too mild a word to describe how she felt. Maybe "loathed" "abhorred" or "despised" would be better. I don't want to go into details, but the evening she first spotted him at the dojo, she stopped me outside and told me she couldn't take this guy. So, in a few minutes, we made a plan of how we could continue practicing together. I was planning on graduating to fourth degree and we needed to find somewhere to practice. She had been going to Sensei West's new dojo about 17 miles west of my house. So, we asked Hanshi if it was OK with him for me to go there too once or twice a week. He was thankfully ok with it, as was Sensei West. Thus began my driving odyssey. I had to keep this all a secret from the Nut, as he would go insane if he knew I was putting so many miles on the car. I would go to Sensei West's for his morning classes once or twice a week and drive home quickly, take a shower, and race back out to my kid's school to pick them up, and then race back home to start dialysis. It was kind of a nightmare. This went on for a few years. In 2011 I did graduate to fourth dan, but I continued at Sensei West's just because I was learning different things there. Fortunately he was kind enough to allow me to attend classes without charging me. Hanshi's dojo was very crowded. So, when we had class it became a case of "the needs of the many outweigh the needs of the few." Karate is kind of like a pyramid; there are fewer and fewer people at the same rank as you the higher in rank that you go. So, most of the time during black belt class, we did Shodan material. I felt like I was stagnating and I wanted to learn new things. So, I continued at Sensei West's for a few years and he even allowed me to bring the kids when they were on breaks from school. My older daughter was right in between his two daughters in terms of age, and they had spent many hours playing together behind the front desk when he was still teaching for Hanshi.

Sensei West's wife was about the same rank as I was when we were going through the kyu ranks before black belt, or maybe she was a little ahead of me. In any case, his two daughters were going through Little Dragons with Natalie at the same time. The Dragons class was right before our adult class. After the Dragons were bowed off, we would install the three girls behind the front desk with crayons, coloring books, and toys to try and keep them distracted for about an hour. I still fondly remember Natalie standing on the corner of the mat one night (she knew not to come onto the mat any further), clutching a crayon, and yelling "DON'T HURT MY MAMA!" while we were sparring. I remember Sensei West telling her it was just "pretend" which it is supposed to be, you are just supposed to have light contact while sparring. She went back to coloring after that, but it was adorable. I think now she couldn't care less if someone beat the crap out of me.

Meanwhile, back at Hanshi's dojo, we changed instructors a few more times. Frankly, I liked all of them after "intolerable man" left. My kids continued to grow up in the dojo and we made the best of the Shodan-heavy curriculum. We did get some of what we needed, and if the kids needed extra help I could always work with them at home. And luckily for me, by 2011 Natalie had become old enough to be my bunkai partner for at least some of my katas. I loved having my two girls as bunkai partners! As Sara got older, I remember she was my "practice partner" at home so when I did practice with Sensei Baylor, I would have most of the bunkai memorized. Of course, she did eventually join Natalie in performing bunkais with me and with her sister during graduations and the Extravaganza.

We continued to progress and by 2015 I had graduated to fifth degree black belt, Natalie who had been junior fourth degree graduated to adult second degree, and Sara graduated to junior fourth degree. I should explain that until a student turned sixteen, they were considered a "junior" rank. The highest junior rank was fourth degree. Both of my girls graduated to junior fourth degree when they were twelve, so unfortunately there was a four year waiting period until they could become adult black belts. However, Hanshi did allow the juniors to graduate to adult second degree (Nidan) after their sixteenth birthday as long as they learned the extra material required. Basically, the juniors were not required to learn bunkais in Hanshi's dojos. So, if they caught up on the bunkais they could pass directly to second degree after they turned sixteen.

I had graduated to apprentice Godan (fifth degree) in June of 2015, and my kids had graduated to apprentice Nidan (second degree) and apprentice junior Yondan (fourth degree) in September. In Hanshi's schools there was a graduation every eight weeks or so. Because there were two dojos, he held the graduations in a church gym that was equally inconvenient for both schools. If you were advancing in black belt rank, you would be awarded an "apprentice" title. Then, in December of every year, we had the Extravaganza, when you would repeat all your material and be awarded your full rank.

Meanwhile, Sensei West had moved his dojo several miles FURTHER away from our house. Now it was taking a solid 45 minutes to an hour to get there. And unfortunately, the Nut had figured out that I was putting a LOT more miles on my car and demanded an answer. I finally had to tell him about my forays to Sensei West's dojo. It was not pretty. But since he had received his kidney transplant in May of 2014 (and his mood had improved somewhat) it went better than I expected. However, I was still getting tired of all the driving and I was going maybe only once a week. And then in July of 2015 I fell down the stairs and tore up the ligaments in my left ankle AGAIN. I have previously mentioned the whole "cast" incident. In any event, I was just starting to come back to karate around the time my daughters graduated to their apprentice ranks in September.

CHAPTER 9

HANSHI

By 2015, life had settled into a familiar routine at Hanshi's dojo. Wednesdays at 6:30 pm was black belt class. This was the most convenient class for most people, hence it was the most crowded. We had a chief instructor we liked, Sensei Strasbourg. Every other Wednesday Hanshi taught the black belt class; he alternated Wednesdays with his other school further south. Saturday mornings there was a black belt class at 9:00 am but it was hard to get everyone up that early. We always made it in in time for weapons and what Hanshi called "protech" which was basically self defense. About once a month there was a special seminar on Wednesdays, and about every eight weeks there was a graduation.

I didn't realize it at the time, but my two kids had become attached to Hanshi as kind of a grandfather figure. We didn't have any family in the state and since they grew up in the dojo they had come to look upon him as a grandfather figure; strict, a little scary, but also kind. Hanshi had been one of the pupils of Hanshi Robert Trias and he was the final authority on all questions about the style. He had started having a "style seminar" every spring and all questions about kata would be answered. I can't say I thought of him as a grandfather, but more like an uncle. Of course, you didn't want to get him angry because that would have consequences. And sometimes he didn't know his own strength. Like the time he accidentally fractured Sensei Baylor's wrist. Or when he "lightly" whacked my knuckles when demonstrating how to disarm someone wielding a bo with a nunchaku. Ouch. Or when he knocked me out demonstrating the sleeper choke. I remember him ridge handing me in the neck and I thought "oh noo…" as I saw stars, my knees buckled, and everything faded to gray. The next thing I remember after that was waking up and thinking "Why is Hanshi hugging me in front of the class?" Well, he wasn't hugging me, he was holding me up!

When Hanshi would ask if you "knew" a kata, people learned pretty quickly that this was a trick question. If you said you did, he would smile, and tell you to run the mirror image (known as the hantai form). Good luck with that if you haven't practiced it. The correct answer was that you could RUN the kata, not that you KNEW the kata. Another thing one learned to avoid was telling Hanshi "I don't understand how that would work." Whether you were talking about a bunkai move, a self defense, or a sparring move, this was a bad idea because Hanshi would proceed to SHOW you in a very painful fashion. Your best bet was to wait until he wasn't there or wasn't looking and ask one of the other instructors. Everyone who had studied with him had some crazy Hanshi stories. We never thought about a life without Hanshi.

By October of 2015 my left ankle was much better and all three of us were reviewing and maintaining our material in preparation for the Extravaganza in December. Then one day, Sensei Strasbourg called us in a few at a time to let us know that he was leaving to work at Angie's List. He had children and he needed a job with benefits like health insurance, which the dojo couldn't provide. Unfortunately, it's tough to get rich being a karate instructor. As I had to explain to my husband numerous times, rent has to be paid, electricity has to be paid, there is liability insurance, etc., etc. Recruiting and retaining new students is difficult. I thought Hanshi's schools had developed a "harder sell" over the years but compared to one of the local tai kwon do chains apparently we were not that aggressive.

In any case, Sensei Strasbourg was leaving. We were told that Hanshi would be taking over as chief instructor which had its good and bad points. The kids of course were worried because now they would have to always be on their best behavior, but I was glad in a way because now we would have the ultimate authority with us all the time. Of course, we would all miss Sensei Strasbourg but we understood why he was going. And he was going to come in intermittently so it's not as if we would never see him in class again. And we were ok too because by now my two daughters were able to be my bunkai partners for the most part so we could practice at home. And I could also help them with their material if Hanshi focused on the Shodan material. It was often hard to retain people past Shodan so it seemed to us that we were left to our own devices sometimes a bit too much. The problem is that people think once they get their black belt, then they're "done." In reality, there is no "done" in karate.

There are ten ranks of black belt but to get to tenth dan you have to be a grandmaster, or hanshi. And to reach that level you have to be active in the style for over fifty years. It's like being a physician, you are always learning, there is always some new material to learn and be tested on.

CHAPTER 10

RONIN

So, the kids were very sad about Sensei Strasbourg leaving. He was really good with children and they had become attached to him as he had been the chief instructor at our dojo for a few years, I think. Then the Saturday before Thanksgiving of 2015, everything changed. I was feeling a bit guilty that morning since I had skipped the graduation on Wednesday. One of the joys of being extremely near sighted is that as you age, you start to have problems seeing at night. I have trouble seeing the lines on the road if there aren't enough street lights. And by November, it starts getting dark pretty early. I had been to every other graduation that year and in general I skip the ones in winter when it's DARK and the weather is worse. And down by the church where we had the graduations it was really dark. I remember thinking "UGH, no... just no." Now I regret I didn't go that time.

I had gone to the dojo that day with only Sara, who was twelve at the time. Natalie, who was sixteen, had stayed home with a cold (even though I had my doubts about her "illness"). We came in with all our gear and our Eikus, since that was the weapon everyone was studying that month. I remember bustling past the offices and I briefly noted Mr. Hamilton sitting with Sensei Strasbourg through the office window. As we plopped all our stuff down in the women's changing room, Sara said, "I saw Mr. Hamilton in the office and he was crying!" I replied, "Well, Sensei Strasbourg is probably telling him that he is leaving, but you might be wrong about the crying. Grown-up men don't cry because their Sensei got a different job. Maybe he has a cold and his eyes are just red." Then Sensei Strasbourg popped his head into the doorway (the changing room doors were always open unless someone was changing) and told me he had to tell me something in the office. I said "oh, you already told us about your new job, that's ok." But he said, "No, it's something else." Sara started to follow me to the office and he stopped her, saying, "no it's only for adults this time, Sara." I remember looking at her and shrugging my shoulders as I walked toward the office, wondering what the heck could be so important that Sara couldn't hear about it. I remember sitting down in the chair and he handed me a paper. It was a letter from Hanshi to everyone and as I started reading it, Sensei Strasbourg started talking. The school was closing. Thoughts were racing around in my brain. We would have the choice of going to Hanshi's other location (a fair distance away, reachable by highway) or going over to Sensei Joseph Williams' dojo, which was much closer. Honestly, I knew how it would have to be almost immediately. I couldn't pick everyone up from school, get them fed and changed, and down to the last of Hanshi's dojos in time for class. I had known Sensei Williams for years, and my girls knew him and liked him too. Every year when we had the style seminar in the spring we would make sure to attend his session on finger locks. So, even though it meant a big change, I felt like it was the better choice. Unfortunately, that was not the end of the news.

Sensei Strasbourg took a deep breath. "there's been a tragedy." I thought he was joking. I remember smiling slightly and saying "a TRAGEDY?" I was upset about the school closing, of course, and about the prospect of having to leave Frank Blair's Karate but I wouldn't classify it as a TRAGEDY. What he said next, however, left me stunned. "Hanshi is dead. He passed away early Friday morning." Now I understood why Mr. Hamilton was crying. At first I was just shocked. I couldn't find any words as Sensei Strasbourg continued speaking. The dojo was going to stay open until the Extravaganza, then it was shutting down. It all kind of hit me and I started crying. Of course there were no tissues in the office and I was wiping my eyes on my gi jacket. Trying to push it down because there was a big window where everyone could see me, and I had to go out and face Sara. I was trying to figure out what to do in the next few minutes, let alone the weeks and months to come.

Now one thing you learn to do in medical training is to "push down" personal feelings. It's kind of a coping mechanism so you can get through, do the work at hand, and (hopefully) not kill anyone. Of course, this is also why there are so many physician suicides. And I had pushed down a lot over the years. Crazy mother? Push it down. Fiancé dumping you long distance, and then learning it was because he was already seeing and had impregnated some college drop out? Push it down. Crazy husband who

harangues you? Push it down. Think about it "later." So I
called on all my skills to push this down for now.

When I left the room, Sara of course wanted to know
what happened. It was time for weapons class, so I just told
her, "Well, unfortunately the dojo is closing but I'll tell you
more later." She started to get upset, and I said, "It will be
ok, we can go to Sensei Williams', I'll tell you after class."
The other (few) people in the class had already been told
of what happened and it was obvious that no one really
wanted to be there. I said, "let's just go through the rules
for the theory in kata and call it a day." So, that's what
we did. I think it was a fifteen minute class that day for
weapons. Back in the changing room I asked Sara, "do you
want to stay for protech or just leave now?" and she wanted
to leave so we did. I asked her if she wanted to get lunch at
the Mexican restaurant in the same strip mall, but she did
not. It had been our habit to get lunch there almost every
Saturday for years. I often wonder if the people who worked
there figured out what happened or if anyone told them.
Because we used to come in our gis straight from karate,
we really stood out.

Somewhere in there I got a call from Natalie. I had been
thinking of how I was going to tell her about everything,
but one of her friends at another dojo beat me to it. When I
answered she said "WHAT HAPPENED TO HANSHI?!
Is it true??? Gail just called me!" Through gritted teeth I
told her "I'll tell you when I get home. We're leaving now.
Don't say anything, let me talk when I get there." I wanted
to tell Sara in the best way I could, I didn't want Natalie
BLURTING it out the minute we walked in the door. I
was thinking and thinking on the way home; I'm surprised

I didn't get into an accident. When we got home, I sat Sara down at the kitchen table and told her that there was more bad news. That Hanshi had died. She burst into tears and I just held her close. I hadn't been sure how she would react. That's when I started to realize just how much he meant to my kids.

The next few weeks and months were a horrible blur. Sensei Strasbourg called me at home and told me when the memorial service would be. It was somewhere relatively far and on a weeknight. And there was more bad news. The owners of the strip mall would not allow the dojo to stay until the middle of December when the Extravaganza was to be held. Everyone was counting on the dojo being open until then and now it would be hard to practice. The dojo's last day was to be the day before Thanksgiving. So, I had to break these new developments to Natalie and Sara. I remember saying "it will be ok. We can practice together at home. I will go to Sensei Williams' after the memorial service and see if we can go there before the Extravaganza." I remember telling the Nut about the memorial service and he replied "It's too far!" I just told him "I can't not go. I have to go." I told the kids they didn't have to go since it was on a weeknight. Much to my surprise, however, they insisted on going. So we went.

The church was packed but we were lucky enough to get a parking spot because we got there early. But there was already a line out the door when we arrived. Hanshi wasn't there physically but the line was to walk past a large photo of him and his gi jacket, belt, and kamas which were framed together. Then to speak briefly with his wife. Seeing his gi jacket and belt, which we had seen him wearing for so long, was very moving and sad. After speaking briefly with his family, we went to stand at the back because we had to leave before the service would be finished. The place was full of adults and children. Most of the kids were crying, including mine. It was more of a "celebration of life" than a funeral, with the high ranking black belts of our style and other styles telling stories about Hanshi. It was sad and funny at the same time. After an hour, maybe longer, we had to make our way out. It was dark by then, and as usual I got lost, even with the GPS. It's tough when you can't see well and we were out in the countryside with poor lighting. I did my best not to freak out because I didn't want to upset the kids any further and eventually we got back home.

The last day at the dojo was rough with people crying throughout the class. I think someone took a picture of us, but honestly I never saw it and with everyone crying, I'm not sure I want to. We were all trying to reassure each other that everything would be OK. I remember Sensei Strasbourg telling us that in the next few months we would be meeting new people, and learning new things. I thought "but I don't want to!" But we had no choice really. It was a difficult class. And we still had the Extravaganza to get through. I had hoped that it would be cancelled because it would be more of a funeral than anything else. But Hanshi's family and the high ranking black belts in our system decided that Hanshi would want us to go on with it. Maybe they were right but it was not going to be like a "normal" Extravaganza.

Once the door closed that night I remember thinking, "that's it. Now we are really ronin. No master, no dojo." We lost a lot of people from our Shorei Goju Ryu community after that and especially after the Extravaganza. Many people just couldn't go on after that. Obviously everything was going to change. But I knew I wanted to continue and I didn't want Natalie and Sara to forget everything they had learned growing up in the dojo. I felt then, and I still do, that Hanshi would want us to go on and continue our journey in the martial arts.

So now the problem was practicing before the Extravaganza. I had talked it over with the kids and they agreed with me that getting over to the last remaining Frank Blair's Karate location would be really difficult after school. It was being run by Sensei Dalton, who they loved, but it would be really a stretch to get there in time for class. So we decided together that we would try Sensei Williams' dojo. I couldn't bring myself to go over to Sensei Williams' until after the memorial service. When I did go, I think I sat in the car for about fifteen minutes before I could bring myself to go in. Immediately I was struck by how dark it was and how much smaller it was than our previous dojo. But, I was here now. I just plopped in a chair by the door. There was no office and I was really struggling not to cry in front of the class that was in session. I got the information and told Sensei Williams and Sensei Benson (who works with him) that we would like to join. They were going to have to increase our monthly dues from what Hanshi was charging us but I was ok with that. Bills have to be paid, after all.

So after that, we all came in together for a class. Thankfully there were several other "refugees" there from our old dojo. We needed a place to practice other than the living room. We had to practice our bunkai, and weapons can take up a lot of space to practice, too. It was weird, as it always is when you go to a new place. New people, new surroundings, new routine; it can be very disorienting. We were facing the opposite direction from the old dojo, meaning that when we bowed in and out the class formation line was on the opposite side. Previously the mirrors were on the north side of the dojo, now they were on the south side. And the windows were now to our left when we did kata, where before they were on the right. I know it sounds silly, but it takes some getting used to. But we only had a couple of weeks until the Extravaganza so we had to "push it down" and get on with it. So we tried our best. It was a big change. As I said, it was smaller. The mat was different. It was darker with different lighting. There was no women's changing room, and only one small bathroom. Sensei Williams uses a lot more Japanese terminology than we did at Hanshi's dojo. But right then we just had to concentrate on getting through the Extravaganza, so we focused on that.

CHAPTER 11

THE EXTRAVAGANZA 2015

I was very apprehensive when the day of the Extravaganza arrived. I was not looking forward to this day at all. We were going to see a lot of our friends again, but everything was different now. It had been decided that Mr. Bob Hudson was going to be our new Hanshi because that was what Hanshi had wanted. We didn't know him very well; in fact we only knew a little about him. We didn't know how he was going to run the Extravaganza. We didn't know what was going to happen. I just remember telling the kids "we just have to do our best and get through this." I still thought it should have been cancelled or turned into another memorial, but this time with all of us wearing our gis.

We got there early, as we always did. I needed time to get all my braces on and the kids like to socialize with their friends from other dojos, although they weren't looking forward to that as much this year. Obviously, of all the dojos in the Shorei Goju Ryu system, we were hit the hardest by Hanshi's death. He was our instructor and our dojo was now closed. Students at the other schools obviously knew him from seminars, tournaments, and the Extravaganza but we saw him every week. He was our teacher.

I was fine and held myself together until we reached the gym itself. Every year the Extravaganza was held in one of the area schools, but it still always involved a highway drive. I don't remember now, but I think the weather was ok that year so there was no snow to worry about. In any case, I was ok as we walked into the school and back to the gym. We were greeted by Hanshi's wife when we went to sign in. I thought that was brave of her. Then we walked into the gym and the kids ran to the back to the bathrooms while I went to find a chair so I could put my knee braces on. Then I saw that they had placed the large photo of Hanshi and his framed gi and kamas in the back, on the stage at the back of the gym. It was at that point that I lost control and started to cry. I found a seat and I was putting my braces on, aware that people were seeing me cry. I tried but I couldn't stop. Sensei Dalton came over and tried to comfort me a little. I wasn't sure I could do this. I had to push it back down so I didn't upset the kids. Finally I got myself together. I saw that the kids were out of the bathroom so I snuck around past them and went in there and washed my face. Sensei Baylor was in there too, but she was doing better than I was. Honestly, I thought the whole thing was horrifying. How could we get through this?

The memories of that day are kind of a blur. I remember making a fair amount of mistakes. Hanshi Hudson was running it a little differently and we got a bit disoriented. Especially for the kata Neko Budo (or Buto). It was five shorter katas which we were used to running as one big long kata and he had us stop between each one. So that threw me off for sure. Emotionally I was OK until he started talking about Hanshi at one point. I remember thinking "NO DON'T GO THERE PLEASE!" But he did and that's when people started crying openly. And when Hanshi Hudson had trouble holding back the tears things got really emotional. Sigh. As I predicted, it was like a funeral in many ways. I remember the video tribute to Hanshi and many of the important masters speaking about him again. And then after that, the diplomas were going to be handed out. We had to line up by dojo and initially we were all confused about where to go, but we ended up lining up for one last time as our Frank Blair's Karate dojo. We took a few final pictures together with Hanshi's picture and then it was over. I really felt like we were ronin then. There was hugging, crying, then saying goodbye. It was a feeling of profound sadness and being a little lost. But somehow we got through it.

There has been a lot of crying since then. I think I have grieved more for Hanshi than for my own father. Maybe it's because I have not lived on Long Island since 1987 and we weren't that close. But, Hanshi we saw every week. It's been hard for the kids, too. As I mentioned previously, Sara has quit karate (hopefully temporarily) because of his death. It's been hard on everyone, but maybe more for my two kids since we didn't have any family in the area. Many people just quit after that Extravaganza, leaving karate altogether. Some have gone down to Sensei Dalton's dojo and some have gone to different styles not affiliated with our Shorei Goju Ryu family. It's sad really, like seeing an extended family breaking apart.

CHAPTER 12

WE START AT WILLIAMS MARTIAL ARTS

The next week I think, we officially started at Williams Martial Arts. As I mentioned previously, it was definitely different than our old dojo. Sensei Williams uses more Japanese terms. I often remarked when there was some word we didn't know that "we were a simple folk over at Frank Blair's Karate. We didn't use such fancy Japanese words." We're still learning over three years later now. I still feel like a newcomer.

There were a lot of other differences, besides the use of Japanese. We had always had a series of "self defense patterns." First there were eight. Then Hanshi took out number three and number eight and he made number seven the new number three. I remember that time because it had taken me SO LONG to learn number eight. I said "Hanshiiiii! (Insert whiney voice here.) It took me TWO MONTHS to learn number eight!" And he replied laughing, "That's why I'm taking it out! It takes people a long time to learn it!" Agree or disagree, that's the way it was. When Hanshi decided something, that's the way it was going to be. And he was the LAW. He wanted things done a specific way every time. Sometimes he would make small changes to a kata and I would joke about "what's the fashion this year for the kata?" One example in particular is Dan Enn Sho. It seemed like at the end of the kata one year we would bring our "dragon tail" (right arm) down into our left PALM, and the next year we were told to bring it down on the DORSUM of our left hand. Sigh. Sometimes this would lead to long searches through and discussions of some obscure point in The Pinnacle of Karate. The Pinnacle was and is our Bible. Written by Hanshi Robert Trias, it has directions and instructions for many of our kata. Hanshi Trias was one of the pioneers of karate in the United States. According to the Pinnacle, he "introduced either Karate-do, sport Karate, or the use of martial arts weapons, both in this country and in many foreign countries."[3] It has gone through I don't know how many editions. But ultimately Hanshi was our style head and he could make changes and we had to follow his instructions.

In any case, back to the self defense patterns. At Williams Martial Arts we have NINE. We're back to the original eight plus one invented by Sensei Williams. But some are different in big and small ways. I still struggle with number five. I understand the WHY of the changes, and I agree that most of them are an improvement. But it's hard to change after fifteen years. But I keep working at it. Overall, there's

---

[3] The Pinnacle of Karate, page 18, Grand Master Robert Trias, 2005 edition.

a lot more room for "individuality" at Sensei Williams', but most of that is because it is a smaller dojo. Hanshi's school was like a MACHINE with many students, and everything had to be taught exactly the same every time because there were so many students. That's just the way it was. We can ask many more questions at Sensei Williams'. There's more time for explanations and debate since it is a smaller dojo. Such as the now infamous Neko BUDO or Neko BUTO kata. The Cat like Warrior or the Dancing Cat? The world may never know.

There were many "rules" at Hanshi's schools regarding how things were taught. There were also rules regarding how one became a sensei. When I started, once you reached Sandan (third degree black belt), then POOF you became a sensei. Then Hanshi started making rules about how many of each different class you had to teach and so by the time I reached sandan there were many rules. Now, I was and am always happy to help out and to teach people, but I wasn't really concerned with having the title of "Sensei." Also, I don't really like following rules which I feel are not important. So, under Hanshi's system, I wasn't a sensei. When we started out at Sensei Williams' dojo, I had just promoted to fifth degree. He started calling me sensei and I thought he was just being polite but finally I told him, "Sensei Williams, I have to be honest. I never fulfilled all Hanshi's rules and requirements for sensei, so you don't have to call me that." But I didn't realize that Sensei Williams didn't follow Hanshi's rules in this, and other matters, so in his dojo I'm a sensei.

Another big change was now we were learning finger locks from small circle jiu jitsu. I watched a number of videos of Professor Wally Jay, who was the originator of small circle jiu jitsu and I learned about the "dance of pain" first hand. This continues to be a work in progress but it's still a big hit at the style seminar. However, now that we're at Williams Martial Arts, I'm helping to instruct. At one of our seminars, Sensei Williams heard a student from another dojo speaking with her friend and saying, "Oh, that's the FINGER MASTER" as he walked by. So, since then, one of his titles is "Finger Master." So, Hanshi Hudson is the overall grand master, Hanshi Roberts is the Weapons Master and Sensei, actually Kyoshi I think, Williams is the FINGER MASTER.

CHAPTER 13

MORE CHANGES...

Over time, Hanshi Hudson instituted more changes. Or I should say, "additions." I should also clarify that when I talk about "Hanshi" I mean Hanshi Frank Blair. When I mean Hanshi Hudson, I specify Hanshi HUDSON. To continue; we added Nai Han Chi Ni and San to our kata list. I'm still working on those. And the biggest change is to the kobudo, or weapons, program. Hanshi Roberts was made our new weapons master by Hanshi Hudson. Before Hanshi died, he did a graduation where if you had graduated to level three in all six weapons, you received your "kobudo" patch. This meant you demonstrated manipulations, free exercise, body conditioning, self defense, and theory in kata. This was basically inserting the weapons into our empty hand katas. Since my girls and I qualified, we received our patches. That was now considered "level one" and we now had traditional katas added to the program. To get to level two you have to learn a traditional kata in three weapons and for level three, you need to perform one in all six. Hanshi Roberts has been appointed our new weapons master, as I mentioned earlier.

He is another very high ranking black belt and also a friend of Hanshi for many years. I was both happy and unhappy. Happy because I had been bugging assorted senseis for YEARS to teach me some traditional weapons katas and we had done some in seminars, but you really need the spaced repetition to LEARN a kata. So I was happy about that. I was unhappy because the lazy part of me was feeling, well, LAZY.

Overall, however, I like learning and I have enjoyed learning the katas. Except Eiku (oar). In general, people either LOVE Eiku or HATE it and you can put me in the HATE group. It's not just because, as someone said, "It's hard to look cool carrying an Eiku." Let alone people yelling at you as you walk through the parking lot "HEY, WHERE'S YOUR BOAT!" Ha ha. I remember when I started in 2001, and when I began learning weapons a few years later, we had FIVE weapons. No Eiku. Then, first Hanshi added the escrima sticks for a while. Then, that was OUT, and we got the OAR. From the very start, I looked at it and thought, "Man, I don't like this thing." I don't know why, but I just don't like it. Of course, we can't forget the great splinter infestation of 2009. The Eikus we all bought turned out to chip and splinter really easily if you practiced self defense with them. When people struck them together, that's when it happened. Everyone was getting splinters, especially the kids (including my own). I remember I donated two tweezers to the dojo. Personally, I came up with the idea of taping the edges of the oar with clear packing tape, which seems to solve the problem. So, overall, I'm not a fan of the Eiku. But I'm learning it because I'm a little OCD and I won't feel complete until I do. I also understand how it is useful to learn to use and manipulate the Eiku. I understand the concept that there are many objects in our environment that are basically a stick with something on the end (i.e., a shovel or a rake). In addition, I won't feel complete unless I am able to earn my level three kobudo patch. In 2018 I was able to graduate to level two and I'm hoping to go to level three this year (2019).

By the end of 2016, Sensei Williams had decided to allow Natalie to graduate to adult Sandan or third degree. This was a pretty big deal because normally you need to wait two years between second and third degree, and Natalie had been an adult Nidan or second degree for one year. However, she had been learning karate since she was three years old, and she had done the obligatory four years sitting at junior fourth degree, since she graduated to that rank at age twelve. I was really happy about this because she was going to graduate high school in about six months and once that happened, she wouldn't be able to come in for lessons regularly, so it would be nice if she reached Sandan before college. The 2016 Extravaganza ran pretty well; there was less of a funeral air about the whole thing. So overall, it was less stressful for Natalie, I think, even though she was graduating to Sandan. It was still all a bit sad though. But life goes on, I guess. We were still trying to adjust to life at our new dojo. Most people kept their "Frank Blair's Karate" patches on their gi jackets, myself included. I don't think that I will ever be able to replace it no matter how much time passes.

I think it was in late 2017 or early 2018 that Sara told me she didn't want to do karate anymore. I was very sad about this for a long time, and I still am. I understand her reasons;

she missed our "community" and it wasn't the same. I get it. But there wasn't much I could do about it, then or now. She had grown up in Hanshi's dojos and I can't bring them or him back. I wish I could.

So, I've been going on my journey alone for the most part since then. Sometimes Natalie comes with me when she's on break, and that's a treat for everyone, I think. Now that Sara is in high school, I'm at the dojo almost every day they are open. Not that I'm the greatest of students, but I figure I'm getting better by osmosis. I'm studying tai chi with Sensei Williams too, but I have to confess I'm a pretty terrible tai chi student. Compared to karate, it's slow, really slow. And I'm no speed demon, either. I can't get the breathing right, because it's opposite (I say "backwards") from karate. Often I can feel my mind wandering and then I get lost. Maybe it's more like microsleeps. I'm not sure I'm improving, honestly, but guilt mostly keeps me going.

CHAPTER 14

MY DREAMS COME TRUE! (AT LEAST ONE OF THEM)

So, over the years I have been asking (or harassing) different instructors about learning some knife throwing or throwing stars. I remember Sensei West talking about "drywall issues" when he turned me down. I don't know WHY, but apparently Hanshi had some objection to people throwing sharp objects in the Dojo. I know I asked a few more people over the years with no better luck. Well, finally my dream has come true. Sensei Williams has granted my wish! He said if I could figure out how to protect the wall and floor, I could do it. So I got this huge piece of not wood, some other type of synthetic material from the hardware store. I can't remember what it's called. And Sensei Dillet donated a piece of pine. I had originally bought a target but it ended up not working that well. Anyway, I bought some knives and stars online and we were in business! We put the protective layer in back, leaning against a shelving unit. Then the pine board in front of that, some cardboard to protect the floor, and we're ready to go! I have since added some throwing spikes, at the suggestion of Sensei Benson. And it turns out, Sensei Dillet is a throwing MASTER, but I also refer to him as "Master of Sharp, Pointy Objects." We've been throwing things for a few months now, and I'm still not very good at it, but I keep practicing and hopefully I will someday be able to kill someone from across the room (just kidding, I think.) At least maybe I can start a new career as a senior citizen ninja. But the cracking noises from my knees and ankles might spoil it. It might make it difficult to sneak up on someone.

The throwing of pointy objects is open to all adults and basically anyone over 16. I was worried because I don't want any of the kids to get any "ideas" and injure themselves, so I hide the pointy objects up on a high shelf behind Sensei Williams' desk.

This story wouldn't be complete without a few words about the Crispy Bacon Ninja Warriors. We have several boy scouts at Sensei Williams' dojo and at some point they had to name their troop. Well, given their karate background, they named themselves the Crispy Bacon Ninja Warriors. When their patches were made, they designed them with a picture of a slice of bacon, wearing a ninja mask, with two nunchaku under its "arms." Sensei Williams said we could add the patches to our uniforms if we wanted and I said, "I'll take me one of those patches!" So I sewed it on and Natalie wanted one too. Of course Sensei Williams has one also. Now whenever we all go to a seminar or the Extravaganza, we all wonder if Hanshi Hudson is going to notice them and what will he say if he does! We're such rebels and troublemakers! I love it!

CHAPTER 15

ALPHA AND OMEGA

So, there we have it. That's the story of my journey in karate so far. I still consider myself a beginner in many ways, especially compared to all the people who have been training for thirty years or more. So I feel like the "alpha" part of the story is still going on. The "omega" is the end of this book, but not of my journey in karate because there is no end in karate. As I said before, it is "the way" or "the path" and there is always more to learn. We can learn within our style and from other styles too. It's been a long road from staring into the window of that dojo in Long Island on my way home from school. Some parts I wish hadn't happened. But Sensei Williams says, "You are where you are supposed to be." I probably never would have been in Shorei Goju Ryu world if I hadn't ended up in Illinois. You see, our style is based here, because that is where Hanshi was from. So who knows if I would have ever ended up in the martial arts. As I said previously, the saying goes "When the student is ready, the master appears." Who know what would have happened if any one of a number of variables had been different.

I hope with telling my story that people, and especially women, of a "certain age" consider studying the martial arts. Don't be discouraged by your age, your weight, or your family obligations. You can do it. Visit different dojos and try to evaluate their philosophies regarding "mature" adult students. If you go in and all you see are a group of 20-something guys beating on each other, that may not be the place for you. If you see some people about your age, you can ask to take a few "trial" lessons. Most dojos will allow you to do this. I remember at one point we had a fair number of "middle aged martial artists" and someone suggested we change the name of the dojo from "Frank Blair's World Champion Karate" to "Frank Blair's MAMA" (for Middle Aged Martial Artists). I'm not sure how Hanshi would have felt about that!

If you have kids, see how they are with children, too. After all, the family that kicks together, sticks together. It is a great activity to do with your children, especially when they are young. The younger you can start them, the better. When they are young, the thing they want most is TO BE WITH YOU. YOU are the center of their world, especially moms. Take advantage of that because you will make wonderful memories that you will keep even after they start to distance themselves from you during the teenage years. Believe me, I speak from experience here. And don't quit when your kids inevitably move on. It will be hard at first (again I speak from experience) but you will still have your karate family with you. Keep learning. If nothing else, you will keep your brain and your body active. And hopefully, in time, the kids will return to the martial arts.

I am sure many of you are wondering what is going on with my husband and I. He is somewhat improved, personality wise, and he is now approaching his five year anniversary for his kidney transplant. He has, occasionally, started a "harangue" or two, which I now quickly shut down. Natalie is off at college, and Sara will be 16 soon. I don't have to worry as much about upsetting them by arguing. He doesn't harass me about karate anymore, maybe because he's too scared now. I don't know what the future holds, honestly. We will see. Stay tuned, because maybe in another eighteen years I'll write MAMA: Part Two!

So, I keep on working, and trying to improve. Hopefully I am. I still have some of my old "squad" from Frank Blair's Karate. And we continue to try to adapt together. I think we drive Sensei Williams and Sensei Benson crazy because we are still having problems learning (or rather re-learning) the self defense patterns and bunkais. As Sensei Strasbourg said, I've met new people and learned new things. But a profound sadness remains for what would have been if Hanshi were still alive. I try not to think about it too much because it still makes me cry. Every day that I go to the dojo, I look at his picture and wonder if this is what he would have wanted for us, his students. I can only hope that he is happy with what we have done and what Shorei Goju Ryu has become, and what it will become in the future.

Printed in the United States
By Bookmasters